Neapolitan Skies

Bernadette Anderson

Neapolitan Skies

Acknowledgements

The following poems have been previously published:
'Tongue Travelling': *InDaily* online, January 17, 2018
'Sinners Wall': *tamba*, Issue 59, 2017
'Frontline': *The Mozzie*, Volume 26, Issue 10, November/December 2018
'Where the Whistle Blows': *Milang Station Chapbook*, 2018
'Duckpond at Dusk': *The Mozzie*, Volume 25, Issue 6, August 2017
'Blue Wheelbarrow': *The Mozzie*, Volume 26, Issue 9, October 2018
'Milang Shacks': *Milang Community News*, February 2018
'Neapolitan Skies': *tamba*, Issue 62, 2018
'I Held a Turtle': *Milang Community News*, December 2016
'Mothers Don't Cry': *Poetry Matters*, Issue 32, March 2018
'Threads': *Poetry Matters*, Issue 32, March 2018
'Fading': *The Mozzie*, Volume 26, Issue 2, March 2018
'My Garden of Memories': *The Write Angle*, Edition 58, February 2017
'Broken Wing': *The Mozzie*, Volume 25, Issue 10, December 2017
'Squeeze': *Poetry Matters*, Issue 32, March 2018 and *The Mozzie*, Volume 26, Issue 3, April 2018
'When Day Becomes Night': *Mindshare* online, 2017
'Ladder of Fear': *Mindshare* online, 2017
'Imposter': *tamba*, Issue 60, 2017
'Memories Afloat': *Milang Community News*, July 2017

For Mum who still guides me,
and for Jessica, Daniel and Timothy
who continue to inspire me.

Neapolitan Skies
ISBN 978 1 76041 763 5
Copyright © text Bernadette Anderson 2019
Cover images: Angela Stephen

First published 2019 by
GINNINDERRA PRESS
PO Box 3461 Port Adelaide 5015 Australia
www.ginninderrapress.com.au

Contents

Tongue Travelling	11
Sinners Wall	12
Happy Chaos	13
Roaming	15
Concrete	17
Seaford to City 18680	18
Car Envy	19
In Receipt of Another's Life	21
Vale	23
Frontline	24
Where the whistle blows	27
Duck Pond at Dusk	28
Autumn Dry	29
Blue wheelbarrow	30
On the move	31
Pruning	32
I Found a Poem	33
Milang Shacks	34
Neapolitan Skies	35
I Held a Turtle	36
Petrichor	38
Shhh	41
Mothers Don't Cry	42
Almost Heaven	43
Nanny and Hayley's Day	45
Hands of Time	46
Fading	47
Black and White	48
Broken Wing	51

Squeeze	52
Overstay	53
Stoking the Flames	55
Suit of Velcro	56
Pretty	58
Naked	59
Bad Mother	60
Threads	62
Diced Memories	63
Scarlet River	65
Bracelet	66
Recalled	67
Spoken Smiles	68
No light	69
When Day Becomes Night	70
Ladder of fear	71
With Practice	72
Takeaway	73
Good Friday	74
Under the Tablecloth	75
Remembered	76
Life With a Dog	79
Dogs and Horses	80
All About You	82
Dog Underneath the Stars	84
Looking for Theo the Terrier	86
Pillow pet	87
Four o'clock…	88
Negotiating Life without Ruby	90
Initiation	93
Breakfast After Trackwork	95

The day Storm Joy ran in the Adelaide Cup	97
Storm Joy	98
Horse Tale	99
Winx	100
Stockwhips and Velvet Noses	101
Grass Stains	103
After the Races	104
Missing What's Missing	107
There will come morning…	108
Imposter	109
When Angels Visit	110
Watering the garden	111
Pink Sheets	112
Late	113
Catch of Breath	115
Love Letter to Mother	116
Memories Afloat	117
Thanks	118

In three words I can sum up everything
I've learned about life: it goes on.

Robert Frost

Tongue Travelling

Some people talk.
Some people listen.
I listen to others share their stories.
Irene from across the cross the road
loves to tell of her grandson's
life on the pearling boats
in the sparkling waters off Broome.
I walk past a woman pruning her roses.
She offers me a glimpse into
her life of home in Sweden
where summer days linger
and snow falls thick and deep and glistening.
Lucy, the check-out girl from the supermarket
is off to South America for her uni gap year.
She is already exploring
the awe-inspiring Inca city of Machu Picchu.
A couple at my local shopping centre
have travelled from the other side of town
for the simple pleasure of a nice drive
and change of scenery.
A walk in George Street Park
finds me shaking hands with an Indian man
who tells me of his new life in Australia.
He smiles and talks of kaffir limes and jackfruit.
Yes, some people talk,
while others prefer to listen.
I like to feel myself woven
into the colourful fabrics
of others travels.

Sinners Wall

Evicted as you take time out
and your lungs become full.
You puff away without a care
hugging sinners wall.

Unlikely to occur, still,
you brace yourself for a fall.
But he has got your back,
that guy sinners wall.

Against blustering winds,
covered in steel wool.
But you cannot hide your sins
when you reside at sinners wall.

There will always be someone who sees you
against hedge, tree or balcony wall.
You will always be sinners in their eyes,
leaning against sinners wall.

Who is left to pardon?
Who is at your beck and call?
The only one who doesn't judge,
that malevolent, sinners wall.

But those who judge are sinners,
the biggest of them all.
For it is they who put in place
that monolith, sinners wall.

Happy Chaos

I sit and observe,
coffee going cold.
So many people.
So many signs.
Lights and shop ornaments
shine and flicker.
Crowds hover around stalls,
wasps' humming encircles a nest.
Bright colours of shop fronts.
Trolleys bursting with groceries, toys
and Christmas wrap.
A living kaleidoscope of colour and movement.
Bags, prams.
Coffee brewing, fresh pastries from the bakery,
perfume, aftershave, body odour.
Manic.

I'm in my comfort zone.
Still I sit and observe,
coffee finished.
Endless queues.
Impatience.
Tantrums from adults and children alike.
Stress overflowing like a bag full of parcels.
I seek out the crowded places.
I feed upon the panic of last-minute Christmas shopping.
Elusive items.
Feet in thongs, flats, heels and wedges,
summer sandals, comfort shoes.
Tattoos on ankles,
slogans on sneakers.
More and more people
invading the store.
Mobile phones ring out.
Children cry.
Frustrations heightened.
Finally, I step in to the slipstream
and I am one
with the chaos.

Roaming

I walk these streets
I've left behind.
I visit neighbours
no longer mine.

Avenues and lanes,
I walk them all.
And still find my way to
this red-bricked wall.

Memories follow me.
My hunger is my pain.
For all I wish is
to go home again.

So, for now
my steps lead me blind
to this home
I've left behind.

I walk these streets
I've left behind
and visit neighbours
welcoming and kind.

Though I dwell at another,
my roots shallow in ground,
I feel like a drifter
who is nowhere bound.

Though distance grows
and days become long,
my steps proceed to
where my heart belongs.

And I continue to find
there are some places
we never can
quite leave behind.

Concrete

Step
by step
  by
     infinite
       step.
Nothing but
  squares of
    concrete
      ahead.
                Bleached.
                Mossed.
                Straight.
                Cracked.
                And grey.
                Everything is grey.
                Ashen.
                Oyster.
                Slate.
The lines are blurred.
My heart is beating much too fast.
I find myself on a conveyor belt.
Steps collapsing onto one another.
                I slip underneath,
            becoming one
                with the grey
      and
    finally
I can
breathe.

Seaford to City 18680

I lie in bed
listening.

On the half hour
I hear the signals
halting the sparse traffic
of late evening.

Buses, cars.
Obedient, waiting.

I hear the train heading north
into the city
hugging the tracks,
rattling
until it is hushed by distance.

But most of all
I listen to the 11.30 p.m. from Seaford,18680.
It arrives in the city at four minutes to 12.

I hear the train and
feel comforted,
knowing it is the final train of the day,
taking people into the city
and returning them.

Then I close my eyes
and await the sounds
of the
train passing.

Car Envy

I have car envy.
I see in other cars
what mine does not possess:
sunroof
sleek body
leather interior
mags
metallic paint to collect and reflect light.
Silver Mercedes with
plush seats, leather this and that
or the blue Mustang with iconic
horse mascot,
push-button ignition,
electric bucket seats,
walnut panelling and dashboard trim
or a black Honda – sporty and sexy.
Yes please.

My car is silver,
with scratches above the hub caps,
plain with faded upholstery.
Inside you will see crumbs
and Allens lolly wrappers
left from a day out with family;
hair ribbons and a blue rabbit
left by a granddaughter
who fills the car with laughter;
dog hair on the back seat,
sand and mud tracks from
dirty sneakers
and tissues for those days when…
bumps and miles are covered
for travelling with big hopes
for small adventures.

If others could look into my car
and peer beyond
wrappers, ribbons and granules of sand,
perhaps they might have
car envy too.

In Receipt of Another's Life

An empty table at last.
I sit with my coffee,
noticing a strip of white paper.
I sigh at another's laziness to
take their rubbish with them.
Curiously I pick up the paper and
read the contents of a receipt.
It is from the newsagent.
Two items paid for with cash.
A book on baby care and a copy of
Marie Claire.
I check the date and time
on my phone and
realise the items were bought this morning,
less than 30 minutes ago.
I wonder at the person who sat here.
An older person perhaps,
not comfortable paying with a credit card.
Or someone like me who likes to have just a small amount
of cash on them for coffee and magazines.
Did you shop for your daughter?
For a younger relation?
Or are you a woman with child?
Perhaps you sat here,
belly protruding, feet aching.
Maybe you did not look at the book,
content to sip a hot beverage,
glancing at your magazine instead.

Maybe you had a small child with you
and had to hurry,
attending to your demanding child's needs.
Then you may have driven home,
putting your child down for a nap.
Next you sat at your sunny kitchen table,
hot drink before you,
as you slowly pored over the magazine
putting the baby book aside for later.
You sigh,
then smile as you feel
little butterfly movements
of the little bud
inside your tummy.

Vale

For Gillian Rolton, 1956–2017

I cried for you
though I never met you,
never looked into your eyes or hugged you tight.
I felt such sorrow wash over me like a hurling wave,
until I felt drowned inside.
I read every piece of comment and obituary about you.
I clamoured for newspaper cuttings.
I remember hearing you speak
at the primary school behind my house one day.
You introduced your champion horse Fred
and the kid's laughter wafted over the fences into my yard.

What makes us grieve for a person we never knew?
What makes us feel broken?
You gave us dreams that we felt we could reach.
You gave so much, dear Gillian,
to your sport and to everyone who knew you and of you.
Vale, Gillian Rolton.
I hope you have returned astride your beloved Fred
to race the wind
and jump floating obstacles
without fear of tumbling.
Vale, equestrian icon.

Frontline

Unresponsive…
Take to bed number four, no five, no take any…
ECG needed…
Heart rate falling…
Where's that blood I took…?
Machines squawk.
Boots and converse sneakers hurry back and forth
under hospital curtains,
squeaking on polished floors.
A voice over the speaker notifies
of incoming patients.
Amongst the panic
a wavering voice asks
if she could sing
her song.
'Go for it,' is the reply.
After a hesitant cough,
sombre and gentle words tell of
'My sweetheart so blue',
my sweetheart so blue',
as the singer is rolled out of the ward,
down the corridor.
Her endearing words
leaving the theatre of war
a little more
serene.

In all things of nature there is
something of the marvellous.

    Aristotle

Where the whistle blows

In 1884 the first trains arrived
to the sleepy town of Milang
on the banks of Lake Alexandrina.
They linked with paddle steamers,
transporting goods between
rail and pier
by horse-drawn trucks.
Passengers sat in carriages,
peering out from windows,
mesmerised by the view of blue lake with pelicans,
bouncing on the waves.
The line connected Milang to
the pretty town of Strathalbyn
passing paddocks of dense scrub.
The last train left the station in 1970.
But if you stand on the wooden platform,
and peer between the gaps of the carriages
at the hazy blue lake,
you can hear the conductor blow his whistle,
and feel the rumble of the train,
as the old Milang railway
comes to life
once again.

Duck Pond at Dusk

                Khaki, pungent water.
Laconic breeze   shepherds ripples   across the pond
        Into   the   bay.
  The water catches   slivers of light,
    filtered through boughs   of surrounding eucalypts.
  Two wood ducks   sit on top of the water;
white bellies and   speckled brown plumage.
Other ducks squabble, bedding   down for the evening,
hidden in spindly   reeds and lush grasses.
Receding waters expose   cracks in bed of green slime,
            roots, rocks and debris.
  Small bob of head   as turtle paddles
        into the centre of the pond,

                                leaving
                                a trail
                                of ripples
                                in
                                his
                                wake

Autumn Dry

The calendar reads April
yet blue skies speak of summer.
Leaves are slow to turn.
Branches split, limbs falling.
Dams are drying, ponds slowly dying.
No quenching rains to fill rifts in soil,
or to soften parched lawns.
A cooling evening breeze the only comfort
as we await heavens waters
to heal the scars of summer.

Blue wheelbarrow

I have a new wheelbarrow.
Steel blue,
it stands
alongside
a mottled grey
shed.
Sometimes
I put it to use,
ferrying leaves, bark,
needles and twigs
to and fro.
Other times
it is enough
for me to admire
my wheelbarrow
alongside
the mottled grey shed.
Though it is not a red wheelbarrow,
glazed with rainwater,
my wheelbarrow
is enough
to make
my
garden
whole.

On the move

Magpies strut,
dignified soldiers on parade.
Pigeons scuffle,
little feet hurrying under grey plumes.
        Fairy-wrens hop and skip.
        Starlings dive and dip.
Noisy Miners hassle,
bullying birds into line.
Galahs waddle with pink bottoms,
plumage splendid in grey and white.
        Swallows hop and skip.
        Sparrows dive and dip.
Yet in the distance, they are alike,
flying a seamless horizon.
On gentled winds,
        they dance to the
                music of the sky.

Pruning

Tending
blood-red roses.
A cut bleeds.
Metallic red on
suntanned arm.
Blood trickles to a stop,
clumped on the end
of its short journey.

A thermometer
filled with mercury.
Dries wrinkled
like paint.

Spirited.
Impassioned.
Sexual.
Brilliant in its hue.
Nothing compares
to the red,
red,
red stain
of blood.

I Found a Poem

I came across
a tree with an umbrella of
lime green leaves
and pods of
peach-coloured berries,
sticky with ants.
I broke a stem
and took it with me.
Layer by layer
I peeled apart the stem,
till I reached the heartwood,
the very centre of its whole.
I breathed the sour notes of sap,
the branch reduced
to a thin fibrous strip,
a bone.
A naked version of myself,
stripped bare before the mirror.
Little remained of the original stem
and yet it was still
a thing of beauty
and wonder
and I realised
I'd found
the
words
to this
poem.

Milang Shacks

Under a bleached sky,
rows of small coloured houses
line the margin
of the bay.

Reedy smell of the lake
draws my eye to the pier
standing on mudflats
lined with salt bush,
and samphire
alight with small white flowers.

Below the calm facade of Milang
on the face of a great lake
the shacks are a string of coloured beads
on the neck
        of shore.

Neapolitan Skies

A late afternoon walk with dog.
I'm caught in the low light
between dusk and sunset.
Falling light shines on two gum trees,
street bound, glowing.
Transfixed
I watch the light
as it levitates before trunks,
alabaster skin tinges pink.
Sunlit clouds ashen grey, pink and white
against a backdrop of soft blue sky.

Ruby pulls at her chain so we walk on.
By the time we arrive home
the sun has fallen from the sky,
although clouds retain their shape and colour,
reminding me of scoops of gelato.
Slowly
light melted
all around
and
the day
closed as gently
as it
had
begun.

I Held a Turtle

I held a turtle in
the palm of my hand,
above his glass house,
webbed feet paddling the air.

I was amazed at
the hardness of his shell
for one so small.

Searching deeper, beneath
the clear waters of his domain,
I imagined open seas in murky darkness,
full of debris.

Sea creatures
from the pristine deep
caged and restrained
in mere puddles.

Looking further
I was amazed by
the erosion of beaches,
slowly decimating habitats.

I cry as the media show
giant turtle cousins
looking on helplessly,
entangled in fishing nets,
slowly starving to death.

I rage at the notion
that we think ourselves clever
because we clone and reshape,
resize and recolour.

And still we sail ships
on wavering seas
that will one day engulf
the largest of its denizens.

I held a turtle in
the palm of my hand.

Petrichor*

On its way.
The sky heralds its coming.
A wavering sun shines meekly
through clouds
draped across
a darkening horizon.
Ants busy themselves in manic lines,
birds riot in the trees.
Washing is urgently gathered off swinging lines,
bundled into wicker baskets.
A scent of fermenting fruit fills the garden.
I hear the gentle pitter-patter of drops
against the window,
slowly building into a crescendo
of rhythmic, beating drums.
Rain has arrived.
Rain has arrived.

* The distinctive smell given off by the earth, rock or pavement at the beginning of a rain after a period of warm, dry weather.

My family is my strength and my weakness

Aishwarya Ra Bachcan

Shhh

Shhh now.
All quiet I beg
for baby is down
in soft-bedded sheets
and pretty nightgown.

Shhh now, shhh.
Nanny's little angel
has finally found sleep.
And so on soft toes
I must gently creep.

Shhh now.
As Fleur De Lys plays on
and winking stars appear,
darling baby's legs lay still
knowing Nanny stays near.

Shhh now, shhh.
Hush the dogs
and quiet the phone.
Leave baby to rest
in her war-safe zone.

Shhh now.
Gentle the door
so baby wont wake,
the sound of beating hearts
the only sound we need make.

Mothers Don't Cry

As mothers, we create excuses
for those times in our lives,
when we feel our pain unravelling
and instinctively push it aside.
>It's just a touch of hay-fever,
>or make-up in my eye.
>Because everyone knows
>mothers don't cry.

All my growing years
I rarely saw my mother cry.
For all that she suffered
she kept the pain inside.
>We keep our troubles to ourselves
>and hold our heads high.
>Because everyone knows
>mothers don't cry.

So, don't be troubled my child,
if you see droplets in my eye.
Its hot today, don't you think?
This heat has made me tired.
>So, one last time
>forgive me one little lie,
>as I turn my back on you,
>and with my face
>against my sleeve,
>softly cry.

Almost Heaven

You walk the edge of the bay.
Waters that take,
do so by stealth;
quiet, unassuming.
The bullying kid who sits in
the front row
of the classroom smiling.
The cat who purrs
and sits on your chest,
claws ready to pierce you.
The swimming pool.
Calm and dozing.
All you see is blue.
Hypnotising blue.
Then you notice her,
face purple,
floating on her back.
Quickly you act,
pull her baby body from
the crocodile infested waters
before they can swallow her.
You can't breathe.
You lie her on her side,
she vomits mouthfuls of water
and
looks up at you as if she has just
woken from sleep.
Now you breathe.

Years that follow
you stand at the edge of the pool
the river's mouth,
with false bravado
and defy them to try again.
Blinking away tears
your body
trembles.

Nanny and Hayley's Day

There's a warmth that remains
long after the embers have died.
A day with granddaughter spent
playing and laughing.
A broken saucer, wet clothes after
playing in the dog's water bowl.
Lightning tantrums when the laundry trolley
is stuck in a groove of concrete.
Sunbeam-smiles when Nanny plays silly games,
bringing plastic farm animals to life
with moos and baas.
Then cuddles,
big hand loosely holding
a little hand as the garden is explored.
Nanny points out the dainty lemon rose in flower
and birds that land on the edge of the bird bath.
No tears, not today.
Hayley eats dinner at the small plastic table,
feeding most of her sandwich to waiting dog.
She falls asleep on Nanny's lap
and parents arrive late to take
the sleepy bundle of
contentment home.

Hands of Time

My freckled hand encases your
plump little fingers,
safe within my clasp.
I struggle now to hold you,
wriggling and twisting
within my palm
My knuckles now taut, veins raised,
divergent rivers searching hills.
Then all I feel are
the lightness of
fingertips
touching
fingertips
until
you
        are
                    gone.

Fading

I picture myself becoming
just a mother,
lost in my life,
which has become
bigger than myself.
Slowly I fall behind everyone else,
hidden in a haze of memories.
I wonder how my children will
think of me
when I face eternal rest
and ponder as I do,
if they told their mother
how much
they loved her
when
she
        was
                here.

Black and White

A small photo from time long past.
At first, I see the small black and white dog,
remember his coat shining,
diamond white patch on his chest.
Then I notice a young girl,
partly hidden behind
the rainwater tank.
I remember her too,
my old self.
Looking further
I recall the confetti colours
of the lantana,
and oleander petals
in shades of musk and strawberry
against the high metal grey fence.
And yet as hard as I try,
that girl, head tilted
staring at me
remains half out of sight
in black and white.

Miscellaneous is always the largest category

Joel Rosenberg

Broken Wing

Please fix my broken wing.
Be careful with your touch.
I am frightened and fragile
but stronger than my size
and not in need of so much.
Just a flex here,
an adjustment there.
Outstretched,
beneath soft down
as translucent as the wind.
Please fix it
so I can fly
into a
bright
new
day.

Squeeze

Your love
is a toxic vine
winding itself
around me.
Strangling, suffocating.
I push you away
but you return
with vigour.
I place
my secateurs around
our tired stem,
squeezing
the blades together.

Overstay

I lie to myself.
Tell myself you'll change.
One day you'll do as you promised.
But ten years on
I'm still waiting.
The D word hangs between us
like the death of a friend.

I do what I am told;
and hang on your wing of promise.
Tomorrow you will tell her you need to end
this strained separation.
To make it final.
To prove to me you have changed your heart,
that now it lies within another.

It is easier pretending to myself.
I deplore myself for my weakness.
Some days everything feels so right.
Like we were meant to be.
But I'm still deceiving myself –
making excuses for you,
excuses for me.
I give into the loneliness,
needing you with me
while harbouring the pain
of lies and disappointment.
But lies can't hide forever
and excuses have a use-by date.

Flowers and gifts.
Pretty cards with pretty sentiments.
I rearrange yet another suite of flowers,
a bundle of pink and white:
lavender, asters and lilies.

I send you away
and that night
dream of us again.

I realise now that it is easier
to change the flowers,
than the vase.

Stoking the Flames

Bellows pump day and night
keeping sparks of romance aglow.
Each blow a gasp of hope
in the red and gold flames.
Dying and living.
Living and dying.

No commitment from you
yet I wait.

The night watches
over the flame
like the moon,
caretaker of the stars.

Too many stars.
The fire needs more and more urging to keep
it burning.

I find my heart slowly emptying
until
all that is left
is a short breath,
slow in motion,
which fails to reach
the tinder nest
before
it
       dies.

Suit of Velcro

I clip the lead on dog's collar,
leave the yard
to calm the bothers in my mind.
Yet with each step
I feel as if my head will explode.
I feel I am wearing
a suit of black Velcro,
collecting every piece of garbage
strewn in my path.
Wrinkled leaves,
burrs and thorns
adhere to me.
Children zooming on scooters.
Dog pulling relentlessly on her lead.
Dog poop in my path.
I scold the children.
I scold the dog.
I scold the day.
Each step feels as if I'm walking in water,
against the tide.
By the time I return home
I feel agitated and resentful.
I feel like screaming.
I let the dog run free
in the yard,
and slump onto the sofa.
I sit under the veranda
and sigh a thousand sighs.

I sit and breathe.
Slowly inhaling,
exhaling
until my Velcro suit
unravels,
breaks down
piece by prickly piece.
And the calmness of the day
slowly descends around me
like arms
around my shoulders.

Pretty

Sometimes when I cry
I stare into the mirror
and study my face.
My eyes look like golf balls,
enlarged and white,
make-up smudged,
eyeliner running down my face.
A failed beauty queen.
My lips are parted,
then that strange smile,
wondering why I am looking
at myself so intently.
I like that look,
that wry smile.
One of the rare moments when
I think I look quite pretty.
Vulnerable;
the same as everybody else
when
they cry.

Naked

Who are you?
Lifeless.
Thin.
Bare.
No petals to
flutter in the breeze.
No colour to define.
Just there.
Barely there.
Are you shy?
Are you becoming you?
Brave
to be who you are
the way you are.
Naked.

Bad Mother

I am a bad mother.
Very bad
not cool as in *bad to the bone*
but bad,
irresponsible, neglectful, remiss.
That is what the
psychiatrist told me.
A professional so he must know.
What type of mother
doesn't take her child to school?
What type of person am I?
Despite years of fighting for my son
to receive help.
All you could tell me
is that my child suffers from
failure to attend school.
How dare you?
How can you tell me
what I know is true?

My son has autism;
finally diagnosed years later.
And I want you to know
that you were wrong.
You were judgemental, unprofessional
and your words prevented
my son and I from
gaining vital support.
You left us alone to fight for ourselves,
left in the woods to fight our way through
the maze of frustration and hurt.
Even my family didn't believe us.
I cried when I heard the diagnosis.
And my son cried too.
Finally he could be the person he was
without the world judging him.
Perhaps I was a bad mother
because I did not stop the words
spilling forth from
your poisoned tongue.
I just walked away.
I should have stood
face to face with you,
and defiantly
told you that you
were wrong.

Threads

For Tim

Small coils of fibres,
snake like, lying
on the bathroom floor.
Sometimes in a heap of knotted cotton
on your bedroom tiles.
Always on, under and around your desk.
Pick. Pick. Pick.
Strings of anxiety.
I follow a tail of blue and black strands
to pants without legs,
shirts without arms.
Blankets and sheets
with hems undone.
More clothing to buy.
More linen to replace.
I toss the thread in the bin,
when all I really wish
is to be able to connect those threads
and put you
back together.

Diced Memories

I studied my hands,
turning them over
fixated on the red and white spots.
Concerned I walked out the back door,
the screen door not quite
closing behind me,
to where Mum stood
under the Hills Hoist
taking washing down,
folding each item neatly
then placing it in the wash basket
at her feet.
I showed her my hands.
You're lucky, she said,
you have mincemeat hands.
I looked at my hands again and then up at her,
a question in my eyes.
It's OK, she said,
it means you're healthy,
you have good circulation.
Mum showed me her hands.
They were the same.
A strange description I thought then.
But now it's a term I use with my own kids,
red playdough with flecks of white.

Sometimes the oddest memories
can be the most endearing:
just like Mum
under the washing line,
the basket at her feet,
with her
mincemeat hands.

Scarlet River

You slip through my hold
like a river of scarlet,
muted but rushing.

I wrap my arms
around my body,
ashamed of its failure
to fulfil its promise
to you,
son or daughter,
and to me.

I close my eyes
to fuse the tears
that connect to
the river of scarlet.

Burnished water stones
catch in the pockets
of my heart,
rich with love,
sorrow and memory.

Bracelet

Plastic and paper.
Light and delicate on my wrist
yet
only the sharp beak of scissors
could rid me of it.
Name and hospital number inscribed.
No space for emotions.
No room to convey
the heartbreak
of my loss
and the worry I felt,
about what I was losing,
feeling so alone in its new world.

I took the bracelet home
and coddled it protectively.
I placed it gently inside
a brown paper bag,
smoothed over with time,
and placed it inside
with two others.

I then placed the brown paper bag
in my drawer,
as carefully as I would
a baby
in its cot,
forever
        sleeping.

Recalled

Sometimes, as I lie in bed,
illuminated in the dark,
shadows enter my bedroom
through slits of bamboo blinds.
Stars dance, tiny fragments
on floor tiles.
I hear my mother's voice
calling me
repeatedly.
I am a child again.
On shadows borrowed from the night,
my body lifts,
and floats
to my mother's side
once again
as I lie in bed.

Spoken Smiles

I grew up afraid of myself.
Bullied at school,
bullied at home.
Too scared to speak or make a noise.
I remember riding the bus to school,
to the city,
full of city workers and students.
I learned to swallow my sneezes,
breathing in a way that they didn't
make a sound.
I never spoke more than a whisper
except at home or at the stables
where the horses would not judge me
or care what I said.
Over time I learned I enjoy talking to
neighbours, café staff, random shoppers.
I've always smiled a lot
but now I feel a satisfaction
when I can state my Hello's
and receive them in turn.
I have a voice now.
It was hidden
but now it has been released,
like a fledgling
from its nest.

No light

Lights are on throughout the house
yet my bedroom is dark.
I wonder how a sky lit up with diamonds
can fail to shed some light through my blind,
angled slats admitting no light.
I have had a good day.
Everything seemed to be going well
but there are times when I can have everything
and still feel so very alone.
Scared, like a lost child.
I remember the night I phoned Mum from a phone booth.
The night was so black, tar-like,
and I misread the street name.
I watched with tears as her car drove slowly passed me,
rear tail lights fading
as the car turned the corner.
I'm close to tears now.
My eyes are heavy
but the fear of what happens if I let them have their way
keeps them open.
I focus on the black, staring at the lights
flickering through the blind.

When Day Becomes Night

The day is bright
yet I'm sitting on the couch shaking with tears.
The nights demons have followed me into the morning
carrying fear and darkness.
Entrapped by fear
I remember calling out in desperation,
waking myself.
I rolled over, away from the terror
but too scared to sleep,
to re-join the dreams
of people, places and
dark days.
I held out as long as I could, heavy lids
succumbing to the night.
The terror returned without a blink of hesitation.
And now, though there is brightness in the day,
all I feel is dread.
I know the night
has followed me
into the day
with its prickly blanket
of fear and darkness.

Ladder of fear

One way to describe living
with bipolar,
is to imagine someone climbing
excitedly onto a roof,
ready to clean gutters
and prune branches
so far out of reach.
Only then,
for that person to realise
they are afraid of heights,
trapped on the ladder
which helped them reach
their place on the rooftop.
They now are captive,
stuck with nowhere to go
and nothing to feel
but fear.

With Practice

For years I would call out to the night,
trying to break through the wall of fear.
But no one would hear me.
My mouth wide open,
no words bursting forth
only a dry gasping sound.
So I took it upon myself
to practice screaming
as loud as I could
every time the nightmares returned.
Somehow it worked
and now I know that
when I am locked in my own private hell,
enough air comes out to form a word or two;
mostly 'help me' or 'go away'.
Now I can hear myself
when I call to the terror,
and just maybe
another will hear me
and wake me
from my panic.

Takeaway

Walking the streets in the early evening,
the enticing whiff
of meals being prepared and served
steals my breath
and makes my stomach hunger.
Thai, Italian, barbecue;
the smell of roast chicken sings through kitchen windows.
Curry, steak, onions and garlic sautéing.
Street after street.
Chilli, coriander, basil and bay leaf.
Dog pulls on her leash,
always in a hurry,
while I try and stand in one spot
to inhale delicious aromas sweeping
through kitchens.
Memories of home-cooked dinners,
mince and veg,
golden syrup pudding,
roast potatoes, tuna mornay, meatloaf, Irish stew.
Roast lamb on a Sunday night
in the yellow kitchen.
Yellow sunlight,
yellow lino,
everything yellow.
We walk slowly home,
my dog draining of energy,
my minds stomach filling
as I dine on a buffet
of heart-warming cooking.

Good Friday

A quiet walk along sleepy streets;
days like this I revel in the pleasure of peace,
pondering last night's dreams.
Thoughts stir gently
as I skirt main roads and busy streets,
enjoying the laneways and byways
where birdsong rises above suburban din.
I feel like I'm back in the days of old
when weekends were for staying home.
When shops rarely opened
and lawnmowers hummed their pleasant sound.
When children grumbled *about having nothing to do.*
There were chores to do of course and homework.
Sundays were pocket money day
where we would list our wants,
usually in the form of lollies –
my brother John, the only one with a bike,
would cycle to the shops on Bray St
and swap small change for bags of lollies.
We even sung a celebratory song:
it went simply
It's pocket money day, It's pocket money day.
These memories float back to drowsy streets
and families playing together
as Good Friday returns once more.

Under the Tablecloth

Heavy floral cloth
covers the table,
hiding a mystery.
Tempting.
Too tempting.
Quickly,
lifting a hem of cloth
I slide my hand under,
and peek
at tiny pieces of coloured cardboard.
Some joined,
creating
an image of sky,
grassy fields,
a shed perhaps.
I hear voices.
Mother and older sister
are imminent.
I hurry my hands
out from the cloth,
then I watch in awe as Mother and sister
carefully remove the cloth
and bend over the table.
Rows of purple stems become fields of lavender,
silver strands of light are a sunlit stream
running beneath lush green grounds.
Slowly the mystery,
hidden underneath the tablecloth
is unravelled.

Remembered

She lay there for days
on her tummy,
one stubby leg up,
the other stubby leg lowered,
as if dropped
in the middle of a tantrum.
Small and dusty,
chocolate brown,
she waited under the green metal mailbox.
Tattered pink ribbon tied
wrong way around her neck.
I smiled when I again walked past
to find her gone,
reclaimed
by the young children
that live there.

Dogs do speak, but only to those who know how to listen.

Orhan Pamuk

Life With a Dog

I don't need to nuzzle your neck
to remind myself of your scent
of stale clothes and shampoo.
But I do anyway.

I really don't need to look
in to your brown,
lucid eyes
to know that your heart beats only for me.
Yet I do so, happily.

I don't need to ruffle your coat
to know the softness of your ears
and coarseness of your hair.

I do not need
to turn around
to know that you
are there.

Dogs and Horses

Sometimes I imagine my dog as a horse.
I watch her walk,
excitable,
pulling on the lead, snorting.
Bull terrier crossed with Anglo Arabian.
Short-backed and long hind legs:
a sprinting machine.
She's a thoroughbred on her dainty toes.
Head down, neck arched,
my strong arms hold her back.
Tail carried high;
her satin coat glistening brown and black.

Her ears prick
as we head for home.
Finally she gives in to my pleas,
slowing her pace,
neck lowered;
ears swivelling towards me
and to the world around her.
I see myself astride her,
looking ahead from between her ears.
The park beckons for a run
so we canter under trees and over bracken,
slowing to a trot as we cross the sparking stream.
I pull her up,
lead her through the gate into the yard.
With a last glance,
her eyes fix on me
before she slowly walks away
her tail swinging low.
My canine mare saunters to her feed bin,
leaving me with bird talk
as the afternoon falls.

All About You

I squeal in delight at good news,
dancing in the kitchen
and you rush to my side,
tail wagging,
dancing at my feet
thinking it's about you.

As I feed the cats pungent sachets
of minced chicken and tuna,
you appear from nowhere,
your nose straight in their bowls,
as though it's meant for you.

I squat on my heels in the hallway
clicking my fingers,
calling the cat to me.
He slowly saunters my way
then you come careering into me,
the cat vanishes,
my attention only for you.

At the end of a troubled day
I retreat to my study.
You lay on your mat by my feet.
I lower my hand to scratch your ears,
but your head is already in my lap
as though my lap was waiting for you.

Your questioning eyes stare into mine.
Brown eyes full of softness and comfort.
I know that look.
I hear your words
as though you can read my thoughts.

What's wrong?
Offer me some of your pain.
Realise
it's not all about you.

Dog Underneath the Stars

I love it when you tilt your head back,
leaning on my shoulder
when we share the sofa.
We watch my choice of TV program
and you don't complain.
When we share pizza,
you cheekily steal my piece,
scattering crumbs over cushions.

Come night time
there is no warmer body to lie next to.
You move around, changing position until
I hear heavy relaxed breathing
and feel your body finally stilled.
Sometimes I wake to find you gone.
I search the house,
then see you sitting outside
nose pointed towards the navy-blue sky,
counting stars.
I ask you to come back to bed
and you willingly oblige.
Most mornings you stay by my side until I rise.

Sometimes you are gone,
light as a whisper,
I never feel you leave.
I long for you to speak of your dreams,
explain the happiness I see in your sunny face.
For that is where I find the love we share;
in your soft brown eyes,
lids outlined with kohl,
and in the wave of your excitable tail.
I love it when you tilt your head back,
leaning on my shoulder
when we share the sofa.

Looking for Theo the Terrier

Where do you go now that your lids lay low?
Do you look for me as I look for you?
If you were able, would you let me know?
Will I find your paw prints in morning dew?

Do you roll joyfully in fields and furrows,
running, leaving muddy prints behind you?
If you could, would you let me know?
Will I find your paw prints in morning dew?

Now that I can feel you, I already know.
Your spirit is happy, your body free.
With peace, I'm able to see where you go.
You run a triumphant path towards me.

I hold you now, brown eyes liquid and kind
as you traverse the hilltops in my mind.

Pillow pet

I make my way slowly
toward him,
barefoot,
and raise him
off the lawn
from a damp patch
of yesterday's rain.
Turning him over,
I smooth his ruffled fur,
push the stuffing back
into the gape of his neck.
Picking off burrs,
I straighten his black floppy ears,
note the missing eye
and carry him inside.
I smile, thinking of the love
for such a simple toy.
Knowing he will be outside again within days,
I place him in the washing machine
and imagine the look
in the family dogs eyes,
when she sees
her favourite toy.

Four o'clock...

...on an ordinary Wednesday.
The afternoon stands still
as I walk my dog
under the warm autumn sun.
The streets are deserted.
>We own the lanes and
>the sunny pavement.

No need to hesitate at the corner
as no traffic
makes crossing effortless.
George Street Park is vacant.
Green and cool.
No children on swings
laughing and calling to each other.
Dogs behind the high metal fence
are hushed.
>We own the park.
>It's four o'clock.

The sun bounces off white-washed
buildings.
A sleepy blue sky
looks down on us.
Trees murmur to us
as we walk underneath,
our footsteps pad the ground.

No neighbours leaning on fences
sharing gossip.
>We own the fences,
>the gates
>and shrubs which
>flower just for us.
The gate creaks as
we enter the yard.
>It's past four o'clock
>and we own
>the day.

Negotiating Life without Ruby

The first thing you notice is the force of gravity pulling you down till you feel it would be easier to crawl on hands and knees. You still carry her collar in your handbag like a child's toy, in case she needs it. You collect pieces of Schmackos and dog biscuit off the floor, placing them on the counter like always. Your feet stumble over the blanketed dog bed at the foot of your bed, dog treat half chewed – you can't bear to put it out of sight. You walk around in a daze, eyes blurred with the rush of years. She is no longer here you tell yourself and yet you see her everywhere. You pause in the pet aisle of the local Coles, staring at her favourite treats. You still cut off the best parts of your meal to leave aside for her. The leash stays crumpled on the sofa where you left it the night you returned home without her. You can't resist buying her a Schmackos 'Chomp and Chew' long-lasting peanut butter and chicken flavour roll, reminding yourself not to tell your son because he will only scoff. You tell your son about buying her the Schmackos 'Chomp and Chew' long-lasting peanut butter and chicken flavoured roll and he scoffs. Her emptiness fills the house, making it hard to breathe. Time spent in the garden is empty of joy so you rarely go there. You pick up all her toys lying on the lawn, the memories too hard to face. You return her toys to the lawn, knowing memories equal pain, but pain reminds you of the love you have lost. You don't vacuum your car, the pockets of dog hair on the front seat a reminder of a day you want to forget but also remember. The stale smell of her unwashed coat stays with you. And every morning you wake, hoping with hope against hope that she is waiting on her blanket by your bed, ears pricked, waiting for you to ask her to jump up next to her where she still belongs.

And God took a handful of southerly wind, blew his breath upon it, and crafted the horse.

Bedouin legend

Initiation

The year is 1979 and
Air Supply hums on the radio.
The clutch growls
as we labour up the hill
in Mum's old Holden Kingswood station wagon.
Sheoak Road:
an avenue of trees and green,
running alongside the train line
and Belair National Park.
Buildings and a roped riding ring
come into view.
Mum parks the car past the stables,
easier to reverse she says.
In freshly washed jodhpurs
and second-hand riding boots
I walk quickly ahead excited to see the horses.
They are tethered on the block,
tails patiently swatting flies.
Heads in halters being pulled this way and that
by small children eager to pat velvet muzzles.
I am smothered by the familiar scent of
leather and horses,
hay and manure.
Mum makes herself comfortable,
leaning against the car.
(She is allergic to horsehair)

My brothers and I look
for my instructor
and find her
leading lazy Harry:
brown and stocky with a swishing tail.
Lesson time.
I smile big and walk to the ring,
my hands taking the reins.
I climb into the saddle,
sitting atop Harry,
my majestic stallion.

Breakfast After Trackwork

Horses are back in their yards,
fed and watered.
Rugs in place.
Utes and floats
are emptied of saddles,
bridles and gear from
the morning's workouts.
The stable smells of wet leather,
wet towels
and wet sand.

Trainer and jockeys hurry inside
to sit at a cramped table
of breakfast offerings.
Mugs of coffee passed along the table,
tea and hot toast.
Newspapers are spread open,
upcoming weights and fields discussed.

Some mornings I am privy
to this scene;
most days to shy to join in,
however much encouraged.
Instead I busy myself
with stable chores,
sweeping the tack room,
checking feed buckets,
brushing horses
or just dreaming on hay bales
under the morning sun.

Soon bodies emerge
from the boss's house
and the next part
of the day begins.

The foreman tells me the colt
in the bullring needs working.
I gather the stock whip and lunging reins,
and walk to the yearling;
on his way to becoming another
thoroughbred,
tracing the circles of fence
at morning trackwork.

The day Storm Joy ran in the Adelaide Cup

Gary led her up
and Alfie had the ride.
She walked around relaxed,
taking it all in her stride
>Sired by the good horse Ngawini
>who defied his pedigree.
>For he was bred for speed
>yet won at distance with ease.

We thought she was in with a chance
if the rain would stay away.
And hoped she would be like her dad
and find the legs to stay.
>We urged her on with vigour
>but coming down the straight,
>the race was all but over.
>She'd left her run too late.

As Alfie brought her in
we gathered all around
to consider what might have been
the day Storm Joy went around.

Storm Joy

A favourite horse of mine;
a sweet temperament
with a rocking horse canter
when you asked her to go.
Brown coat and brown kindly eyes,
honest and brave and never one to fuss.

Eventually she was put through the sales.
I was there making her coat shine.
I brushed her coat,
running a damp cloth over her shiny hide.
I had her looking like a winner.
She was led away into the ring
and sold for a brood mare price.

The sun then left my sky.
I'm not too ashamed to say
I shed a few tears, later on my own
the day they took my mare Storm Joy away.

I was 14 years old when I learnt
perhaps it's the fate of many,
who do good in their own soft way
that when their life changes,
only those they are closest to
feel the tremors.

Horse Tale

At the back of a warped photo album,
I remove strands of jet black horse hair.
Scribbled words on yellow card tell me
it was taken from a horses rug in 1980.
How quickly I am back there,
standing in his yard,
the smell of hay and manure
rich in my memory.
I brush his heavy brown coat,
rhythmic strokes,
soothing him, soothing me.

Prince Plea, the gentle giant;
a brave horse,
winning on the flat and later over hurdles.
I arrange his heavy rugs for the night,
pulling loose tail hair caught in the straps.
I pocket it in my jeans,
bringing it home where I keep it safe.

Now I comb my fingers gently
through coarse, tangled hairs,
precious
as silk.

Winx

On winning the Bob Ingham Stakes, Randwick, 19 August 2017

The favoured mare missed the start,
giving the field four lengths.
The crowd, given a fright
averted their eyes
in disbelief.
A thousand pair of eyes
looked again as the caller's voice
rang with excitement.
Winx was last at the 600 metres,
her stablemate leading the field.
The callers voice raised an octave
as the defiant mare raced up on the outside,
closing in on the leader.
Could she get there?
Would she keep her winning streak intact?
Like a whirlwind
she propelled herself from
the rear of the field
to grab the line by a half neck.
Crowd roared.
Exalted.
The great mare
is now a legend.

Stockwhips and Velvet Noses

I once lived in a world
where creatures of immense beauty and stamina
galloped, majestic and bold,
across racetrack's
lush and verdant.
These same horses crushed their shoulders
as they fell to the turf.
These horses snapped legs like twigs
as they galloped on the heels of the horse in front of them.
I saw a horse with a metal paling
imbedded in his side
as he tried,
eyes wide with fear,
to jump back into the mounting enclosure.
I have comforted horses returned from a race
with blood pouring out of flared nostrils.
The yearling that was whipped,
blood scarred hindquarters
because she refused to float.
The same weapon was handed to me
to complete the task,
but I could hardly raise my arm,
for fear of hurting her anymore.
Saddle-sore horses ridden day in, day out,
blisters festered and bleeding.
A trembling black mare,
so terrified she was uncatchable,
until I slowly gained her trust
in the small hours when no one was around.

I have known softest velvet muzzles
which reach over the rail
to breathe me,
snorting softly
as they bury their noses
in my hair,
my clothes
and
my life.

Grass Stains

A ride in the truck after dark
to gather fresh grass for the horses.
Grassed stained jeans from dewy lawn.
Mr B is soon on top of me,
makes me promise not to tell.
>	I lie in bed after a full day
>	working at the farm.
>	I close my eyes on hearing his approach,
>	pretending to be asleep
>	as Mr F opens the door, comes to my bedside,
>	touches me.
>	He knows I won't tell.

Gerard has a big beautiful chestnut gelding.
Constant promises of a ride on his horse
as soon as I visit his stables.
I went to his stables
but I wasn't rewarded with
a ride on his horse.
I never told.
>	Gifted a pair of sexy underwear from a stable friend.
>	I was confused.
>	Sexual comments about my body,
>	wolf whistles from men at the track.
>	Still confused
>	with no one to tell,
>	until now.

After the Races

Afternoon closes as we pull into the dusty driveway.
Two floats. Four horses.
Home from a weary day at Murray Bridge.
Horses are unloaded, walked to their yards
where feed of chaff and oats awaits.

There is a gentleness
as we go quietly about our work.
I rug the last of the horses,
check every feed bin and water pail.

Lastly hay nets are filled and hung
with fresh sweet smelling Lucerne.
I check saddles and bridles
for the following morning.

I'm the last to leave.
I run my eye over the comforting scene
of horses content,
soft neighs and nickers,
sounds of munching hay.

Darkness is now falling quickly,
like curtains closing.
I bid the horses goodnight,
and pick up my bike,
handle bars leaving a dent in the fence,
like a thousand hoof prints
embedded on the turf.

Life began with waking up and loving
my mother's face.

George Eliot

Missing What's Missing

No hill to drive down.
No empty car space to locate.
The nursing home doors that won't slide open for me,
I could never remember the code.
The vacancy in your eyes.
The words you couldn't say and the words I struggled to find.
The food you refused and bendy straw your lips refused to grasp.
The chocolates I couldn't wrap for you.
The card I won't spend forever time deciding on,
making sure the words are just right.
Childlike pictures taped to walls I would have smiled at.
This coming Christmas,
my thoughts are
left to dwell
on missing
all that is
missing.
And the mother I no longer have
to share it with.

There will come morning…

For Mum, 1939–2016

and the rituals of the day.
Life will seem no different
though I wish it not this way.

The day then grows long
while I harbour the pain.
And not for the first time
wish myself a child again.

Evening soon comes.
In dusky light birds chorus and play.
With all things a reminder
of why I feel this way.

And there will come morning
as life continues on its way.
Sometimes bringing with it tears
Since you, my mother, went away.

Imposter

For Mum, 1939–2016

For some time, now
I have seen a lady
walking around the shopping centre.
She reminds me of you.
Baggy pink cardigan,
unflattering shoes,
and a face so like yours.
She pushes a trolley
filled with too much for one.
Straggly grey hair, small green eyes
focused straight ahead.
She never looks at me,
yet I cannot help but stare.
I imagine myself walking
up to her and saying hello.
How I wish she was you
but she is not you.
You are not here anymore.
Yet seeing her makes me happy,
if only for a moment
as I picture you
as if you were here.

When Angels Visit

I play a word game on my iPhone
before placing the phone,
screen open,
on the kitchen table.

I search for missing photos.
Later, I open a plastic tub,
find a funeral card with a picture
of my smiling mum on the cover.
I sit in my chair,
holding the card out in front of me.
I cry a little.
Talk to her.
Cry a little more.

Returning to the kitchen,
I read the letters of the word game,
scrambled when I left my phone.
Now I see
the letters of your name,
J O A N
spelt clearly
on my screen.
I look up,
thank you
for staying near
and cry
softly.

Watering the garden

For Mum, 1939–2016

The wrathful summer sun
exits at dusk,
after invading our afternoon.
I find you in the garden,
hose in hand,
watering dry beds of roses,
the dogs weaving between
our legs,
wagging tails.
Mum and I exchange thoughts,
our tongues mute,
comfortable in
this silence.
I'm happy just standing
next to you.
Mosquitoes begin to nibble
on exposed arms;
a sign to head indoors.
I turn to watch you
wind the hose on its
plastic reel.
But you are already gone.
I smile, blinking away tears,
and close
the screen door
behind me.

Pink Sheets

Pretty pink sheets
adorn my bed.
Straight onto the bed,
wrinkled
from plastic packaging.
>   So pale,
>   any more washing
>   would render them
>   white.
>   Pretty pink.
>   I'm that little girl
>   that never had
>   pretty sheets.

In bed
I am
nestled among
rose petals.
At the cemetery
a delicate pink rose
sits in a jar
alongside
mothers plaque
at the cemetery.
>   As the pale rose fades to off-white,
>   I feel mother is finally at peace.
>   A dove set free to fly
>   in a sky tinged with pink.

Late

Running late.
My car parked outside the school.
Running late.
I reach into my bag for my phone to call you.
I delve, scramble, can't find the phone.
Finally I feel its weight.
Running late.
I have to let you know.
I press, repress and stab at the buttons.
Where is your number?
I am panicked.
I have to let you know.
Finally my phone hums
and hums
ringing itself into silence.
It feels like an hour.
Then I realise you aren't there.
You died 12 months earlier.
You died, Mum
and I was calling you to let you know
I was running late.

I wake up then, rub my eyes,
confused at first about my whereabouts.
It was just a dream.
I thought I was running late
but it was just a dream.
Yet I saw you,
looking perplexed
wondering where I am.
I wish I could return
to the nub of the dream
and touch you.

Catch of Breath

I was not there when your day closed
gifting you into the light.
I was not there when your last breath
slipped slowly through your lips.
If I'd known the time of your final whisper,
I would have stood by your side,
small jar at the ready,
to catch those last instants,
to trap the moment's particles
in glass.

Love Letter to Mother

Skin as pale and wan as a fading summer's day. Eyes green/grey as sullen seas, that sparkle like shell fragments under translucent waves. Short bob of glossy brown curls from a do-it at-home perming kit. We would often joke about who was your favourite child, you had ten to choose from. Your reply was a predictable but warming *Come now. I love all my children. I don't have favourites*. And as children we would watch black-and -white movies with you, and laugh as you praised your *Handsome Heroes* of the time. Like these black-and-white movie stars of old, you lived most of your life in the shadows, waiting your turn to shine. How you begged us to be ourselves, never let anyone in who would compromise our being. Yet unfortunately Mother, I failed you. I turned myself inside out for others, and now live with regret. Wordsworth describes beautifully, what could only have been written for you in 'Perfect Woman', the final parable says: *A perfect woman, nobly plan'd, To warn, to comfort, and command; And yet a Spirit still, and bright With something of angelic light.* Now with your passing, your shine is dazzling, as you were when playing your beloved piano, ivories wavering up and down, classical music, magic slowly rising about you as mist above the river at morn. Funny how one recalls such things as I do now, the bitter, unpleasant odour of ammonia as you dyed your hair behind the bathroom door. Your smile, your compassion, ability to be everywhere at once. Mother, I don't know how you did it, but you have shown me that Mothers are miracles. Thank you for still guiding me, reassuring me. I know you're waiting till I sit by your side again to watch those black-and-white movies together.

Memories Afloat

When I think of memories,
I imagine
slivers of silver and blue thread
dangling
like jellyfish
in translucent seas.
Some memories
sink to the ocean floor,
too heavy with pain
to resurface.
But most circle and dance
on foamy tips of waves,
treading water,
until we call them
home
to shore.

Thanks

Thank you to my publisher, Ginninderra Press, for supporting a new writer like me. Special thanks to my editor, the wonderful Jude Aquilina, for first believing in me and convincing me to have faith in myself. And of course, thanks to my children Jessica, Daniel and Timothy for their ongoing enthusiasm, not to mention my granddaughter Hayley who has been a welcome distraction when I needed it most.

To Sue Cook, Linda Balogh, and Colleen and Jock McCallum, all who have read and reread my poems and encouraged me all the way on this amazing journey. Also thanks to Ros Schulz for her support and Angela Stephen for the beautiful artwork.

Thanks also to the staff and tutors at Adelaide College of Arts (Professional Writing), where I first began the ride.

www.ingramcontent.com/pod-product-compliance
Lightning Source LLC
Chambersburg PA
CBHW070922080526
44589CB00013B/1397